Memoir of Mrs. Chloe Spear:
a Native of Africa, Who was Enslaved in Childhood,
and Died in Boston, January 3, 1815...Aged 65 Years:
By A Lady of Boston

James Loring

CHLOE AND HER PLAYMATES TAKEN CAPTIVE BY
THE SLAVE-DEALERS.

MEMOIR

OF

Mrs. CHLOE SPEAR,

A NATIVE OF AFRICA,

WHO WAS

ENSLAVED IN CHILDHOOD,

AND DIED IN BOSTON, JANUARY 3, 1815....AGED 65 YEARS.

BY A LADY OF BOSTON.

———

" To the praise of the glory of his grace."
" If the Son shall make you free, ye shall be free indeed."

———

BOSTON:
PUBLISHED BY JAMES LORING,
132 Washington Street.
....
1832.

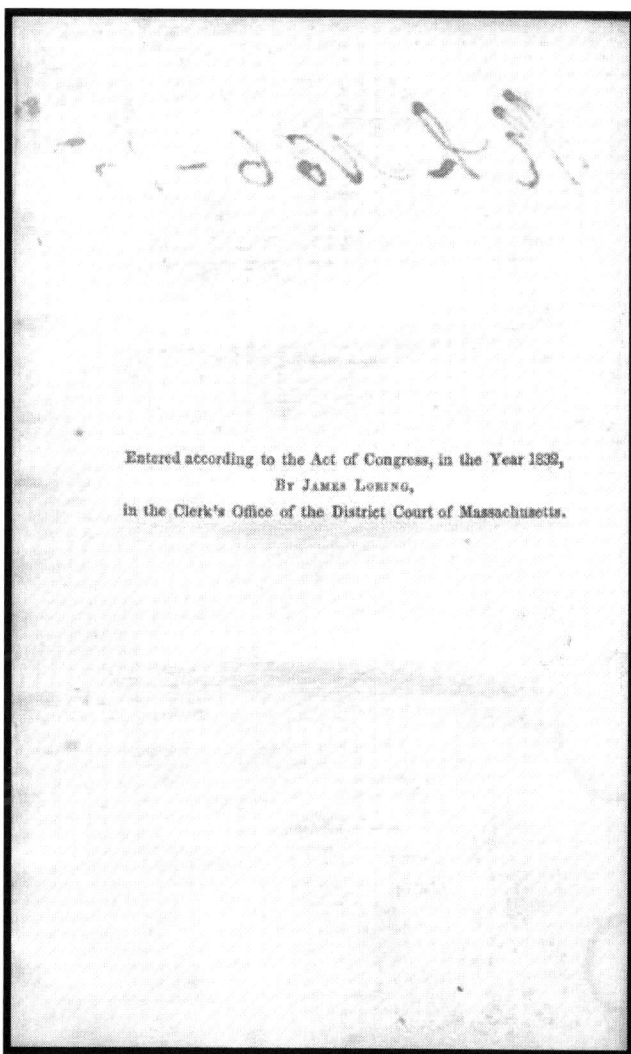

MEMOIR
OF
MRS. CHLOE SPEAR,
A NATIVE OF AFRICA,
WHO WAS
ENSLAVED IN CHILDHOOD,
AND DIED IN BOSTON, JANUARY 3,
1815 .... AGED 65 YEARS.

BY A LADY OF BOSTON.

"To the praise of the glory of his grace."

"If the Son shall make you free, ye shall be free indeed."

BOSTON:
PUBLISHED BY JAMES LORING,
132 Washington Street.
1832.

PREFACE.

When a book is put into the hands of young persons, in the form of a Memoir or Narrative, it is common to hear them ask, "Is it true?" In reply to this interrogation respecting the following little historical sketch, we say, It is true. And other particulars might be related that would be interesting; but as the immediate design of the writer, was to make more extensively known the grace and mercy of GOD, and the power of the Gospel, in bringing the humble individual, whose experience it narrates, to the knowledge of himself; it is thought unnecessary to exceed the present limits. It is sincerely commended to the blessing of Him, who can make the feeblest means instrumental of promoting his own glory, and the salvation of souls. It must be evident that nothing but the Religion of Jesus could have effected such a change in a poor heathen. Such a religion must be worth possessing, for nothing else can renew the heart of the most enlightened individual in refined society.

> "Let the heathen, let the Negro,
> Let the rude Barbarian see
> That divine and glorious conquest,
> Once obtained on CALVARY."

In noticing the dates, it will be perceived that the subject of the Memoir has been dead, a little more than seventeen years. Hence the question may arise in the minds of some, "If the character was so well esteemed, why has the work not been executed before this?" The only reply that can be made to such an inquiry is, no one has performed it, although a number of her friends have regretted that something of the kind had not been done.

Impelled by the persuasion that "whatsoever our hands find to do," must be done, speedily, and supposing that it might never be otherwise done at all, the attempt has thus been made. Not, however, with a view to any pecuniary emolument to the writer,--as the avails of the copy-right will be devoted to the benefit of Schools in Africa,--but for reasons already assigned. A Member of the Second Baptist Church in Boston.

BOSTON, MAY, 1832.

CHLOE SPEAR.

CHAPTER I.

The time and manner of her Capture--Arrival in America--Separation from those who were taken with her--She is sold, and brought to Boston-- Recollection of her native country--Desire to learn to read--Partial success in the undertaking, and subsequent grievous disappointment.

About seventy years ago, on the coast of Africa, the subject of the following memoir, in company with four neighboring children, herself the youngest, according, to the statements from her own lips to the writer, resorted to the shore for amusement, either by bathing in the cooling stream, or other playful sports to which they were accustomed, with the full expectation of returning to their several homes, as usual, after such seasons of childish diversion.

While engaged in these innocent and healthful recreations, they were suddenly surprised by the appearance of several persons, who had secreted themselves behind the bushes: they knew not what to imagine they were, having never seen a white man; from whose frightful presence they attempted to shrink away, but from whose cruel grasp they found it impossible to escape. Not withstanding the piteous cries and tears of these poor defenseless children, they were arrested by cruel hands, put in to a boat, and carried to the dismal Slave Ship, which lay off a few miles in the river, the horrid receptacle of a living cargo, stolen from its rightful soil, by barbarous hunters of human prey for the purposes of traffic. Terror and amazement, as may be supposed, took full possession of their minds. Everything around them was as novel as it was dreadful. A ship, they had never before seen; the language of these strange intruders was perfectly unintelligible to them and their intentions they were unable to comprehend: and no tender mother, no avenging father near, to know or to alleviate their wretchedness. Ah! little did these hapless children realize, when they quitted their native huts and frolicked, away to the woody beach, that they had left, for the last time, the places of their birth, and the fond embraces of their parents and brothers and sisters--that the last parting kiss of maternal affection had rested on their lips, and that they were about to participate once for all, in those much-loved plays which had hitherto been undisturbed and joyous. Little! nay, not at all did they realize, that their hostile invaders lay there in ambush, "like the lion that is greedy of his prey," with ferocious intent forever to deprive them of all their domestic felicities, as dear to them as to the rosy children of America. But, alas! such was the fact. We can better conceive than express the feelings of their parents and friends when night came on, and the looked for children returned not. Silence --silence has ensued, from that to the present hour. From their injured children, they heard no more. The bitter wailings of a bereft mother, the deep anxiety of an afflicted father, the tender lamentations and suffused eyes of brothers and sisters, were utterly disregarded by

those inhuman wretches, who had plundered them
of what they held so dear.

But, ah! that was not the end of the matter.
When that solemn day shall arrive, when, as
foretold in prophetic vision, "The dead, small and
great, bond and free, shall stand before God," and
be "judged according to their works,"--then, a most
fearful account, which is now sealed up to that day,
must be given, even by the most hardened of all
God's vast creation. Nor can we refrain from
observing how far do those portions of the human
family who can thus wantonly injure the
defenceless and ignorant of their own species,
degrade themselves below the unhappy objects of
their unkindness, and even below the beasts that
perish. No creature so unwise, none so irrational as
those on whom their Creator has lavished the
greatest amount of intelligence; none so unkind as
those, whom he has rendered the most capable of
kindly affections; none so unhappy as those, whom
he has best qualified for the enjoyment of
happiness, who yet abuse his favours! How
ungrateful is rational, civilized man! Did he act
agreeably to the powers and advantages with which
he is endowed, he would every moment be
increasing his own happiness, and that of his
fellow-men, by the exercise of gratitude, the
application of wisdom to those noble purposes for
which it is given him; and a tender regard for the
rights of others.

The cruel separation being made, and the terrified, weeping victims packed on board the floating prison, her sails are bent, and she bears them from Africa's romantic wilds, never to return. The spot, however, from whence they were stolen, is still a part of this "dim speck call'd earth," and will testify against the perpetrators of the dreadful deed.

The length of the passage is not known; the end of the voyage, however, brought them to Philadelphia, in the state of Pennsylvania, a portion of our country rendered sacred to liberty, by the "friend," whose name she perpetuates,--WILLIAM PENN.

Here, another painful separation was to take place. Hitherto the children had remained together, nor does the writer recollect to have understood that they were beaten, or otherwise cruelly treated, as many others have been. But now they were to be disposed of like cattle taken to a Fair, to the highest bidder. At the time they were exhibited in the market, the subject of our little history, whom, she said, the sailors used to call Pickaninny, on account of her being the smallest of the lot, was sick; consequently she did not meet a ready sale. The others were sold, she knew not to whom, and carried she knew not whither. To one of them she was more particularly attached, and suffered severely on her being taken from her. She herself, was subsequently purchased by Mr B. and brought to Boston, Massachusetts. Foul stain on the character of our beloved New-England! Thus divided from all she held dear in this life, and knowing nothing of a better, she sighed, and wished for death; supposing that when she died, she should return to her country and friends. This imagination she derived from a superstitious tradition of her ancestors, who, she said, supposed that the first infant born in a family after the decease of a member, was the same individual come back again, just as they saw a young moon appear after the old one was gone away.

She did not know her age, but from her appearance she was judged, she said, to be about twelve, at the time of her arrival. But, young as she was, she remembered various particulars respecting her country, such as climate, fruits, traditions, &c. And having always been accustomed to warm weather, she could not be made to understand what was meant by winter; and when told that, at that season, water sometimes became so hard that it could be cut with an axe, she was astonished and quite incredulous. When winter came on, and she first saw the falling flakes of snow, she was highly amused and playful. And as the season advanced, and produced to her senses the solid ice, she found, by ocular demonstration, that the assertions she had heard were indeed true!

She remembered the Tamarind tree, and other productions which grew spontaneously, and in rich abundance; but these, although so useful when brought to this country, as she herself witnessed, were useless to the natives, because they were ignorant of their nature and qualities, and also of the means and methods of improving them to their comfort or profit.

Although enlightened and good people must always have known, that it was a barbarous and wicked thing to take their fellow-beings from their native land, and bring them to ours, to sell or buy them for slaves; yet it is well known that then there was less knowledge of its wickedness than there now is. Hence we are willing to believe, that if the master and mistress of this poor, oppressed girl, whose story is here related, and whom they named Chloe, had lived in our day, they would have dealt very differently by her from what they then did. But at that time, here, as now in many parts of the world, slaves were considered property, and their owners thought themselves under no more obligations to instruct them, otherwise than to do their work in such a manner as best to subserve their own interests, than farmers do, to take, their horses and oxen into their houses, instead of the pasture or the barn. With such views, it is not singular that Chloe was taught nothing, comparatively, of her duty to God, nor to read the blessed Bible. She was, it is true, sent to meeting half the day on the Sabbath; but the seat assigned to herself and her associates was remote from the view of the congregation; and she confessed, that as they did not understand the preaching, they took no interest in it, and spent the time in playing, eating nuts, &c.

and derived no benefit whatever, though the preaching probably was evangelical.

It was close personal instruction that she needed, to discover to her the beauty of religion, and her condition as a sinner. This she did not receive. But, being favoured by the munificent Author of her existence, with superior intellectual powers, which, if cultivated, would have raised her above many of a different complexion; when, (as she was accustomed to do,) she went to conduct the children of the family to, and from school, she discovered that the were obtaining something of which she remained ignorant. This excited an inclination to learn to read, and after becoming a little acquainted with the school-mistress, who, it would seem, manifested some sympathy for the enslaved youth, she ventured to express her desire.

How to accomplish her object, was a question which required consideration. She was aware that it would not do to make known her wishes at home, and she could not attend at the regular school hours, both for want of time, and because the children would expose the fact to their parents. But after some reflection, an expedient was devised that promised success. "So," said Chloe, "I ask de Mistress how much she hab week to teach me such time I get when school out, and my work done? She say, 'five copper,'*

*This was previous to the coinage of cents.

so she would chalk down mark, how many day I go, till make a week. She say too, I mus bring book."

To these conditions she agreed, as she occasionally received small presents of money from visiters at the house of her master.

Delighted with the prospect, she hastened to a bookseller's shop, and desired him to sell her a book. He asked, what book? She answered that she did not know; she wanted a book. He asked what money she had brought? She did not know this neither, but showing him her piece of silver, he found it to be a twenty-cent piece. Whether the bookseller willingly took advantage of her ignorance, or whether he supposed she was sent to purchase a book of that value, we cannot decide; but he gave her a Psalter, which contained the Psalms, Proverbs, and our Lord's Sermon on the mount. An unsuitable book indeed, on which to teach an untutored African her alphabet! but this event Chloe afterwards had occasion to review as a peculiar providence.

By diligence in her domestic avocations, and so much application to, study as circumstances would permit, she learned her letters, and became quite interested in attempting to spell. She kept the book secreted in her pocket, and whenever she had a few moments leisure, she would take it out and try to spell a word. While thus engaged one day, her master discovered the book in her hand, and inquired what she was doing. She told the truth,*

*She told the truth! What an example is this to all children and youth. Had Chloe done as have many who were better taught than she, no doubt she might for a time, have escaped the reproofs of her master, and possibly have continued to attend her school. But her conscience must all her life long have been accusing her of lying, and this would have been far worse than what she endured in consequence of the deprivation she suffered; for it is better to suffer wrong, than to do wrong. Besides, she would in all probability have been detected at some future period, and then the mortification, in addition to the guilt, would have been a severe aggravation of her punishment. But what is greater than all, she would have sinned against God, and thus have exposed herself to his holy displeasure.

and this led to a full disclosure of the case. He angrily forbade her going again to the schoolmistress for instruction, even under penalty of being suspended by her two thumbs, and severely whipped; he said it made negroes saucy to know how to read, &c.

This was truly an afflictive stroke to poor Chloe, but she was obliged to submit as well as she could, and altogether to desist from going to school. She however hid her book under her pillow, and when not likely to be detected, she used to labour over it, and strive to remember what she had learned, and to find out as much as she could herself;*

*Such patient diligence, and persevering effort, under these trying and discouraging circumstances, discover traits of a strong and penetrating genius, which would be highly creditable to an enlightened student, and most powerfully reprove those children of kind and attentive parents, who are constantly prompting them to the improvement of their minds by personal instruction, and by affording them superior advantages of a literary character; but who are still negligent and remiss in their attention to study.

and years afterward, even late in life, she frequently spoke of it as a striking providence, that the first verse she was able to spell out, so as to understand it, was Psalm xxxv. 1. "Plead my cause, O Lord, with them that strive with me: fight against them that fight against me." She had gathered some ideas of a Supreme Being, and had imbibed a sort of confidence in his justice; and feeling herself unjustly treated by man, she found some consolation in the hope of redress from a higher Power, still longing for release by death. As she progressed in spelling, she perceived that her own feelings were expressed in other passages, particularly Psalm lxxi. 4.

"Deliver me, O my God, out of the hand of the wicked, out of the hand of the unrighteous and cruel man."

By these things she was led to believe, that a kind Providence had placed the scriptures of truth in her way, to be a comfort to her, even in that dark state. Had it been a common spelling-book, instead of a Psalter, she could not have derived this advantage. The spelling-books of that day, it is well known, differed widely in point of religious instruction, from those of a more recent date. Few, if any portions of scripture were inserted. Had it even been otherwise, those of which she here speaks, are less adapted to such a work, than many others. We may therefore safely conclude with her, that it was providential.

How far the passages of scripture she mentions were applicable to the conduct of Mr B. it is not our province to determine; but it is not strange that they should have served to sustain an individual so situated. She felt an ardent desire to learn to read, and that she was unreasonably opposed in this undertaking. It must therefore have afforded a sort of solace to her feelings to find that some one had been oppressed as well as herself, and that there was some ground of hope for her likewise. She appeared, however, not to have possessed, and certainly not to have retained, a revengeful spirit.

The valuable improvement she made of the very scanty advantages she enjoyed, strikingly shows that her master indulged a mistaken idea in supposing that the natural results of education were unfavourable. Education, like health, or property, may be misimproved, and turned to a bad account; but health and property, if rightly improved, are among our greatest blessings, and so is education in all its various grades, as experience has amply proved. And we who are so happy as to live in brighter days, should look back with pity, as well as disapprobation, on those who have erred on this point, and forward, with joyful anticipations, to succeeding generations, while the tide of improvement shall roll on, and its current become more and more broad and rapid, till knowledge, even the knowledge of the Lord, which is the grand climax of education, shall cover the earth as the waters do the sea.

The most direct and certain method of securing to ourselves the reasonable services of domestics, or children, is to afford them such instruction, as will discover to their understandings, the nature of the duties they owe both to God, and man; thus rendering it plain to their perception, that their personal happiness is inseparably connected with their obedience and faithfulness in the fulfilment of those duties.

CHAPTER II.

First serious Impressions--Removal to Andover during the war--Further instruction in reading, by Mr A. of that place--Deep feeling upon the subject of Religion--Return to Boston--Makes a public profession.

CHLOE could give no correct account of dates; but, to judge from other events, she must have become a woman grown, when a female of her acquaintance, who resided in the neighbourhood, was taken very sick; and her mistress sending her occasionally with a little broth, or with something that might be for the comfort of the individual, gave her an opportunity of witnessing, the state of the sufferer. In a short time, while she was one day engaged in her domestic duties, she was informed that the young woman was dying. Having a kind of curiosity to be present on such an occasion, and withal feeling somewhat alarmed, she left her work, and repaired to the house of death. The sight affected her. Death appeared to be something different from what she had been wont to view it. The thought of having so improperly spent their time when they used to be together at meeting, rushed upon her mind. When the spirit had departed, she began to reflect, where is she? &c. And either owing to these circumstances, or to some remark by another spectator, or to both, this appears to have been the first thing that made what may be considered a serious impression upon the mind of this daughter of Africa. She knew not what it was, and had no one to explain it to her, or to instruct her on, the subject.

Not far from that time, and during the American revolution, her master removed his family to the town of Andover, about twenty miles from Boston. As was the case with many other gentlemen, who owned and occupied large and handsome houses in their native town, when, owing to the perils of the times, they were obliged to quit their homes, and take up with part of a house in the country; so it was with the master of Chloe. And this was another remarkable providence, which to her, will be an occasion of devout and grateful admiration forever! He took up his residence in a part of the house of Mr Adams, who was a truly pious and devoted Christian. Thoughts of the dying neighbour, and melancholy reflections about country and kindred, connected with the trials of her involuntary servitude, cast a gloom over the countenance of Chloe, which betrayed itself to the discerning eye of an enlightened Christian, as indicating a sensibility of soul which demanded sympathy. With a readiness to impart needful instruction and kindly consolation, congenial to a benevolent and noble mind, Mr A. manifested an interest in her welfare, and in a very friendly and unforbidding manner inquired of her, "What is the matter Chloe, are you sick?" Unaccustomed to so much apparent tenderness, and not understanding the nature of her own trouble, she felt rather abashed, and scarcely knew what to say but replied in her simple manner, "O, Sir, my mind sick." This language was more intelligible to this Christian friend, than to herself, and he took proper occasions to call her into his room, and converse with her about her soul. A relation of her story, naturally unfolded the incidents respecting her attempts to learn to read, &c. The pity of the good man for this dejected slave, was still more strongly excited. He kindly offered to teach her further, and for this purpose gave her permission to go into his room after her master's family had retired, and her work was finished. She thankfully accepted the offer, considering it a high privilege to have another opportunity to learn to read the Scriptures. She deprived herself of sleep after working hard in the day, that she might gain an object so desirable in her esteem.

In addition to elementary instruction in reading, Mr A. failed not to give her such religious instruction and advice as were calculated, with the blessing of God, to benefit her precious soul, commending her to Him, in fervent, humble prayer. And it now became evident that the Spirit of God was operating upon her heart.

After one of these interesting occasions, being more deeply impressed than usual with a sense of her sinfulness, she returned into her kitchen; and having seen that her fire was secure for the night, feeling herself entirely alone, she fell on her knees, and in broken accents, poured out her soul to God, pleading, as well as she knew how, for mercy and forgiveness.

On rising, she was startled by the voice of her master, who, having suspected that something new was going on, had seated himself in his parlour to watch the movements. "O!" (said Chloe, when relating the story,) "my heart up in my mouth. I di'n know what to do, what I hab to suffer. But I went in de parlour, 'cause he call me. He say, 'Chloe, dis week, you go Mr S. de minister, and ask him baptize you.' I frighten! I say, O massa, I poor creature, I no fit for baptize. 'Yes,' he say, 'any body pray as you hab, is fit.' I 'fraid say much, fear he angry, so, soon I could, I go up my chamber; den I tink, what all dis mean? Same man tell me once, I should no learn read, if I do, I tie up by my two thumb, and whipp'd; same man now tell me go be baptize! What all dis mean?"

Thus unexpectedly brought into a strait, poor Chloe was greatly distressed. When her master called her, she supposed he intended to correct her. That he should, at once, tell her to ask for baptism, was so wide an extreme, she was equally alarmed. Conscious that she was not, agreeably to the views she now entertained of the necessity of regeneration, a suitable subject, she trembled at the idea. But not daring to disobey her master, she complied with his order, and was sprinkled after the mode of infant baptism. This afforded no relief to her troubled conscience; she became more distressed on account of sin; her "heart more sick;" particularly on hearing a sermon on the unpardonable sin.

In this state of mind, she resorted to her kind friend, Mr A. who endeavoured to console her feelings by instructing her, that although she was a great sinner, and nothing but the blood of Christ could cleanse her, yet owing to her ignorance of religious subjects, he thought she could not have committed that sin, and therefore there was hope that she might receive forgiveness, if she truly repented, and came to the Saviour in his own appointed way. Her mind grew more calm, but she did not rest satisfied, until she had reason to believe that she was enabled to cast herself wholly on the mercy of God in Christ, and resign her soul into his hands, for time and for eternity.

What length of time they remained in the country, is not known to the writer; nor is it recollected precisely, that the subject of our memoir arrived at a settled conclusion respecting the important change, above mentioned, while there, or soon after her return to Boston; but some time subsequently to the re-settlement of the family at home, feeling a humble hope in the merits of her Saviour, she believed it to be her duty to make an open profession of his name. This she did by uniting with the New-North Congregational Church, then under the pastoral care of Rev. Dr. Elliot, (senior,) an excellent man, and a faithful preacher of the gospel.

How obvious is it from the foregoing chapter, that the omniscient eye of the great Jehovah is over all the works of his hands. He who setteth up kings, and putteth them down at his pleasure; who made and governs worlds and beings of every order; who has myriads of angels and seraphs around his throne; He who must bow even to behold the things that are done in heaven, --condescended to notice this obscure female, and so to order events in his Providence, overruling even the calamity of war, as to place her under the observation of one of his own beloved children, who knew, from personal experience, the sorrows of a sin-sick soul, the preciousness of the balm of consolation, and the value of the "Physician," who alone is able to apply it. "Surely," O Lord, "the wrath of man shall praise thee, and the remainder of wrath thou wilt restrain!"

Convictions of truth, having been evidently fastened on her conscience by means of the death-bed scene, she needed much of that sort of instruction, which, to human probability, she would not have enjoyed, had she been circumstanced as previously. God is never at a loss for methods and instruments to accomplish his own holy and benevolent purposes. He who notices the falling of the sparrow, and directs the lightning of heaven in its course, led the steps of Mr B. to the habitation of one who feared God, and was not a respecter of persons, and thus opened the way for Chloe to receive unexpected assistance in her efforts to learn to read, and likewise to have the path to heaven and happiness lighted up before her in the blessed gospel.

The momentous change which was wrought in her heart, was indeed effected by an Almighty influence; and was precisely the same as every

genuine Christian, whether a Chloe, or a Hannah
More, a Lazarus, or an Abraham, must, and does
experience, before he can enter a heaven of
holiness; agreeably to the declaration of our Lord,
"Except a man be born again, he cannot see the
kingdom of God." John iii. 3.

How dreadful then will it be in that solemn
day, when we shall all appear before the judgment-
seat of Christ, should any, who may have read this
little history, be found unprepared for his coming,
while this uncultivated African shall sit down in the
kingdom of heaven, with Abraham and Isaac and
Jacob, and all the ransomed of the Lord out of every
nation and people; forever to celebrate Redeeming
Love!

That this may not be the case, let all be
admonished now, while the day and the means of
grace are prolonged, to "flee from the wrath to
come," and seek for a thorough and experimental
change of heart. The following lines are appropriate
to this point.

"Lord, with this guilty heart of mine,
To thy dear Cross I flee;
And to thy grace my soul resign,
To be renewed by THEE." Watts.

CHAPTER III.

Advances in the esteem and confidence of her master and friends--Her marriage--Freedom by a law of the Commonwealth--Prefers to reside with her "old massa"--Occasional attendance on the lectures of Dr. Stillman and Mr. Gair--Unites with the church of the latter--Strong affection for Christians, of whatever denomination--Desire for a home of her own, to receive the people of God --Remarkable industry, by which means she purchases a house--Decease of her children--and of her husband.

CHLOE ever had been, and still continued to be, a faithful servant, and gained the approbation and confidence of all the family, and the esteem of their friends and connexions. While yet a slave, she was married to Cesar Spear, and became the mother of several children.

"As a reward of her integrity, her master gave her a certificate of manumission, (freedom) which was to take effect at a specified period not very distant. But shortly after, by a law of the Commonwealth, all the slaves in the State were made free."[*]

[*] Mass. Baptist Magazine, Vol. of 1815.

It however was her choice, to remain for the present, with her "old massa;" this being mutually agreeable, he thenceforward paid her for her services.

A family-like attachment subsisted between them, to the close of life. The son of Mr B. she used to style her "young massa," and was in the habit of visiting his family after the decease of his parents.

From them she received various marks of kindness, and of solicitude for her comfort, both in sickness, and in health. To the grand-children, it was a peculiar gratification to have a visit from "good old Chloe."

Her stated place of worship on the Lord's-day, was the New-North Church; but as there were no evening meetings held there, she was much in the habit of attending the regular weekly lectures of the late venerated Dr. Stillman, and after the settlement of Rev. Mr. Gair over the Second Baptist Church, she often attended his lectures also, and sought opportunities of conversing with him on the subject of religion. As she became more acquainted with the Scriptures, her mind was gradually enlightened, and after various peculiar trials on the subject, she was, led clearly into the doctrine of believers' baptism by immersion; was, baptized by Mr. Gair, and admitted a member of that church, in the month of November, 1788.

She was ardently attached to the people of God, of whatever denomination, and rejoiced to associate with them in his worship. Particularly was she delighted with the little social meetings held at private houses, where the religious experiences of Christians were often made a topic of conversation, and in which she found her own exercises more fully developed, than she herself was capable of expressing them; and she formed the resolution, that if, in the course of Providence, she should ever be permitted to have a home of her own, she would open her doors for such purposes.

It may indeed be said of her, she grew in grace and in knowledge, and in favour with God and man. Her case was a striking instance of sovereign, distinguishing goodness; and she frequently spoke of it with devout gratitude, that she, an ignorant, defenceless child, should have been taken from country and kindred, and subjected to slavery in a strange land, that she might be made acquainted with the gospel, be redeemed from the more cruel bondage of sin, and brought into the liberty of the children of God. "They," she would say, "meant it for evil, but God meant it for good. To his name be the glory." She no longer desired to die, and go to her native land, but earnestly prayed that the blessed gospel might be sent there, and to the utmost ends of the earth.

In process of time, she, with her husband, commenced house-keeping. But he being of a different turn of mind from herself, and not seriously disposed,--she did not enjoy all the domestic happiness that was desirable. She was enabled, notwithstanding, to maintain her Christian profession with meekness. Having taken a decided stand for God, she kept it firmly to the end.

By habits of industry and economy, she found herself gaining in property; and felt an increasing desire, to possess, some time or other, a little habitation that she could call her own. Stimulated by this desire, she worked early and late though not to the neglect of religious duties, either public or private. A strict and conscientious regard to these, she said, strengthened her, and prompted her to the discharge of her secular duties. She not only assisted her husband in the care of a family of boarders, who were seamen, or labourers, but she also took in washing, and went into various families as a washerwoman, &c. And whatever she could save of her earnings, she carefully laid up.

The families for whom she worked, frequently gave her their cold meat and vegetables, which served to help out a meal at home, and consequently lessened the expense of providing; and as her husband was more particular to have enough to eat, than to inquire from whence it came, and was in the habit of submitting the chief management of domestic affairs, to his "cleber wife," she had opportunities in this way, of adding to her little stock.

After returning from a hard day's work, she many a time, went to washing for her customers in the night, while her husband was taking his rest,-- extended lines across her room, and hung up her clothes to dry, while she retired to bed for a few hours; then arose, prepared breakfast, and went out to work again, leaving her ironing to be done on her return at night. Cesar, having been accustomed to cooking, &c. could, on these occasions, wait upon himself and boarders, during her absence; but was quite willing that she should make ready a good supper, after she came home.

Her husband, although he possessed none of the refinement, or economy, for which his companion was so remarkable, was, nevertheless, fond of finery and show, and would sometimes say to her, "Chloe, why you don't wear silk gown, dress up smart, like udder colour women?" "Well," she would reply, "you give me money, I can buy silk gown, well as any body." The money, he would give to her; but think so little on the subject afterward, that, instead of an extravagant dress, something cheap, and comfortable, satisfied good Chloe, and the surplus augmented her treasury; which, in her estimation, was a thing of far greater importance, than gay clothing. Here the business rested, until he again discovered that she needed a new dress, to make her appear fashionable, when, as before, she managed so judiciously as to increase her fund.

Things went on much in this way, for several years. All their children, one after another, to the number of seven, deceased; only one of whom, it is believed, left any children, and at the time of her own death, her only surviving relative was a grand-son.

For a long time she concealed, within her own mind, the project of reserving her earnings for the purpose, and with the hope of purchasing a little tenement, not knowing what might take place, or whether she should ever accumulate a sufficiency. One day hearing of an unfinished house for sale, she made inquiries respecting it, and critically examined her capital, to see if she might venture to hope for a consummation of her wishes. Having satisfied herself, and being aware that the purchase must be made in her husband's name, "'cause he de head," she said to him, "Cesar, house to sell; I wish we buy it." He laughed at her, for thinking of such a thing, but asked her, "how much e price ob it?" "Seben hundred dollar," she answered. "Seben hundred dollar!!" exclaimed Cesar, "I no got de money, how I buy a house?" "I got money," said Chloe. At first, he knew not how to believe her; having never suspected her plans; but she stated to him the methods by which she had acquired, and from time to time laid up this sum of money. He then was pleased, and very readily agreed to the purchase, which, with the advice of her friends, was soon effected. But the house* was unfinished. She therefore proposed that themselves should occupy the most inferior part of it, and let out the remainder, until, from the income, they could finish one room after another, and thus increase the rent, which, with the blessing of Providence, might serve to support them, should they live to grow old. That also was effected. But during this lapse of time, her husband, after a long and painful illness, was removed by the hand of death.

*The house stands near the head of a lane on the north side of Rev. Mr. Parkman's Meeting-House, in Hanover Street, Boston.

Under this dispensation of Divine Providence, Chloe behaved with much Christian propriety.

The circumstance of dissolving her connexion with the church with which she first united, was one of deep interest to Chloe, as she in a most solemn and impressive manner related to the writer, long after it took place, and as she had previously done to others. With her, it was a subject of much prayer, searching the Scriptures, and close self-examination. It was clearly apparent that she acted conscientiously, and under an affecting sense of her accountableness to God. That she was ardently attached to the people of God, of whatever denomination, was manifest to all who knew her. His people, were her people; she loved her Saviour's image wherever she saw it. And as her discernment of Christian character and experience was keen and discriminating, she was capable of enjoying much in their society; and also of suitably esteeming the privilege of receiving them into her house.

The temper she discovered in relation to her captivity, strongly resembled that of Joseph, whose language she quoted when adverting to the subject. Like her blessed Lord and Master, she breathed the spirit of forgiveness, and prayed for the salvation of those, who had injured her. This must have been owing to the influence of religion upon her heart; and the same influence filled her with thankfulness to God for bringing her to this land of Bibles; enlarged her desires for the happiness of her relatives, and so corrected her views, that, instead of vainly wishing to transmigrate into an infant, and live again in her native country, subject to all its destitution of religious privileges; her constant prayer was, that the light of divine truth might be conveyed to them, that they also, might believe and be saved.

We perceive from the preceding chapter, that she realized her desires with regard to having "a home of her own." Here we see too, the unsatisfying nature of earthly comforts, and how uncertain it is, even if we are brought into possession of what we desire, whether we shall experience all the enjoyment we anticipate. She, it seems, did not enjoy all the domestic happiness that was desirable. While her happiness consisted in quietly communing with God, and her own heart; that of her husband consisted in eating and drinking, and associating with his comrades. This must have been a heavy trial; but it served to keep her humble, and show her her dependance upon God alone, for solid comfort.

Let her troubles and disappointments, teach those, who hear of them, not to depend too confidently on temporal circumstances to render them happy. Our God often sees it necessary to send with our earthly blessings, some trial, for which we did not look, and which greatly embitters our comforts. Were it not so, we should too often rest on them as our chief good.

It is a pleasing trait in her Christian character, that neither trouble, nor hard work, prevailed, to induce in her a relaxation from her attendance on the public means of religious improvement, or the retired privileges of the closet.

Although there are periods in the life of every Christian, when it is more obviously a duty to be engaged in avocations of a domestic or business character, than to be at meeting, or secluded from the family, on our knees; yet it is extremely hazardous to a life of devotion, and no less so to the faithful and acceptable discharge of secular duties, to yield to the idea, that everything of a worldly nature, must be attended to first: and then, if we "have time," pretend to worship and serve our Creator. The Saviour says, "Seek first the kingdom of God." By this he does not intend, that we should spend a great length of time in "making long prayers," but that we should make religion our primary concern, and the glory of God, our supreme and ultimate object. When this is done, our temporal affairs will not suffer for want of proper attention. This we see exemplified in the conduct of Chloe.

The industry and enterprise, which are presented to view in the third chapter of her history, are truly admirable in such an individual. In these, we have a pattern, worthy of the imitation of any class of our readers.

The idea of purchasing a house and land, by means so unpromising, would have appeared to thousands too chimerical to be indulged; too uncertain, to encourage an effort. Many a cool calculating mathematicion, had he been consulted on the subject, would have thought it advisable that she content herself with buying her silk dresses, and living upon the best fare she could obtain; and risk a support, when old age arrived, in the alms-house, or wherever it might happen to be convenient. But Chloe "attempted, expected," and accomplished, "great things;" and, in the evening of life, when no longer able to endure hardships, she sat down to the full enjoyment of the fruit of her labors, and the still richer luxury of imparting a portion to the needy.

One error, however, we must allow that she committed. And, in consequence of this, she probably suffered much, in the latter part of her life time. Her perseverance led her beyond due bounds, in the practice of drying washed clothes in her sleeping room. Though she was insensible of it at the time, it was, probably, laying a foundation for the very distressing Rheumatic complaints, with which she was afterwards so seriously afflicted. Still, we will not be hasty in condemning her, as it is difficult to say what else she could have done, without sustaining a considerable loss. Her customers wanted their clothes in season. She had no other apartment in which it was proper to dry them It was not safe to put them out of doors in the night, as it might be a temptation to someone to take them dishonestly. We must therefore leave the subject as it respected herself, while we cannot hold her up as an example in this particular, because a similar exposure, might prove destructive to health, even where the constitution is good.

Her readiness to deny herself trifling gratifications, for the sake of providing for the future, evinced a strength of mind, not always discoverable in those, whose advantages may lead us to suppose, they have even more moral courage, than one like herself. Her skill and fore-thought, also, in contriving to finish their house, may be advantageously improved by all who are endeavouring to rise in the world, by personal effort. Penetration, Industry, and Economy, exercised in humble dependence on the blessing of Providence, form the grand secret of success in the accumulation of wealth. "The blessing of the Lord," says the Psalmist, "maketh rich, and he addeth no sorrow with it." Let none, then, fail to seek his blessing, when about to engage in the pursuit of lawful undertakings.

The chapter concludes with a brief statement of the decease of her husband. This is the final close of all earthly scenes, to each individual of the human family. Sooner, or later, the solemn change will pass upon all of us; and it is of equal importance, to each, that he be found in a state of preparation for that event. Whatever disappointments may overtake us, in our journey through this vale of tears, no one will be disappointed in the expectation of DEATH. Many, indeed, have, and many more will, experience sad disappointments, in their fond expectations of long life. But amid all the uncertainties that attend the calculations of mortals, no one has reason to entertain the slightest apprehension, that Death will be unfaithful in the execution of his warrant. He never fails to aim a successful arrow at his victim, at the moment he receives his commission to send it! "Death passed upon all men, for that all have sinned."

Under this dispensation of Providence, we have remarked, she behaved with much Christian propriety. She did not make a display of grief, and pretend that she had lost one of the best of husbands, as is the case with some persons after their friends are dead, but who were not very ardently attached to them while they lived. Still, being deeply affected with the apprehension that he was not prepared for heaven, though he had been often warned of his danger, she felt distressed on his account, but believed it to be her duty to bow submissively to the will of her heavenly Father, satisfied that "the Judge of all the earth had done right." She could now, with all her heart, plead for a fulfilment of the promises of God, made especially to the widow, and on him she cast all her care.

CHAPTER IV.

Religious Meetings at her house--Visits of respectable
friends--Description of her person--Disposition --
Benevolence--Interest in Missions--Usefulness --Spirituality,
and Humility--Gratitude for mercies--Sickness and Death.

HAVING realized the earnest desire of her
heart, viz. that she might have a home of her own;
and now having no one to control her, with
inexpressible delight, she set about performing
more fully, her former resolutions, although she had
not been unmindful of them, from the time of her
commencing house-keeper. Her doors were opened
for religious meetings, and many, not only of her
own colour, but also of her other friends, found it
pleasant and profitable, to visit their widowed sister
Chloe, and hold converse with her upon those
things which relate to another and better world. Her
beloved Pastor, the late Dr. Baldwin, the honoured
successor of Mr. Gair, in the oversight of the church
used to esteem it a privilege to participate in
exercises of this nature, under her peaceful roof.
And, occasionally, pious ladies, of the first
respectability, were pleased to make her an
afternoon visit; when, with her accustomed
modesty, she would wait on them, and then take her
own tea by herself. This reserve, however, was in
the course of time, removed, by the affability of her
friends. So true is the promise of God,--"They that
honour me, I will honour." And, "he that humbleth
himself shall be exalted."

Her person was rather above the common size; her countenance open, and interesting; her disposition placid and cheerful, though at a great remove from levity. Her language was extremely broken; so much so, she could never pronounce many words which are in common use. In attempting sometimes to speak, and perceiving by a restrained smile on the countenances of those present, that she was incorrect, she would very pleasantly laugh at herself, with a view to give others the opportunity to do so, without the fear of hurting her feelings.

A disposition to forgive injuries, was also a prominent feature in her character. Of this, a single anecdote is sufficient.--She had experienced from an individual, some treatment, not altogether so kind as she had reason to expect. He subsequently became sensible of his error, and spoke to her on the subject. The readiness she instantly manifested for a reconciliation, produced a degree of surprise, which he could not easily conceal. "Brudder," said she, "don't you know, when any body bow to me, I always drop?"--courtseying down to the ground to express her meaning, viz. that she was willing to take "the lowest place."

She was kind and benevolent to the poor and distressed. Whenever objects of charity were presented, her hand was open for their relief. Indeed, she measured her personal expenses in view of the necessities of others, and used to say, she never felt "stingy," only when she was procuring something for herself. She would then economize, that she might always have something to impart to such as were in want; "especially those who were of the household of faith."

When Christians in this country began efficiently to promote the glorious cause of Missions, her heart exulted in prospect of the enlargement of the Redeemer's kingdom. She longed, and prayed, for the spread of the gospel, and especially that "Ethiopia might soon stretch out her hand unto God." Thousands of her petitions for this desirable object are on file, and will assuredly be answered in the fullness of time. Yea, already, we see evident answers, in the efforts of his people for its accomplishment, and in the blessing which has followed. In these efforts, how sincerely would she rejoice. Peradventure, she does rejoice in them!

Nor did she present her prayers only. Her alms also, are still a memorial before God, and before his people.

Such were her desires for usefulness in the cause of Christ, that she would often say, if he would condescend to let her do any thing for him, she should view it a privilege, were it "only to fill up a pin hole," (alluding to the ancient Jewish tabernacle,) or render the smallest service to his saints. And he was pleased to make her useful, more especially among those of her own colour.

The blessings promised to the "peace-maker" were hers, to a desirable extent. She was peculiarly successful in healing difficulties, even where those of superior abilities had failed. And so happy was her talent in conversation with persons, in the early stages of religious conviction, that in seasons of revival in the neighbouring towns, she was frequently invited to visit them, and was instrumental of good. Perhaps a recollection of such interviews may be revived in the minds of some, who may read this memoir.

But, it was in fervent spirituality of mind, that our friend excelled. The character, and glory of God, the FATHER, SON, and HOLY SPIRIT, and the stupendous plan of man's redemption, were the themes, that most of all, engrossed her meditations, and were the ground of her comfort. Her perceptions of divine truth were remarkably clear. She evidently lived near the throne of grace, and derived her enjoyment from the fountain-head. Her conversation was comforting even to those far advanced in the Christian course; and instructive and pleasing to the young. There was much of life and animation in her manners, and she was peculiar for conveying her ideas in metaphors which originated in her own mind, and thus often engaged the attention, and rendered herself agreeable to persons, who were not particularly serious.

When wishing to state her ideas of the difference in her feelings towards God, as the Author of her mercies, and man, as the instrument of communicating them; she often brought the following similitude: "My mistress sometimes used to send me wid present to lady; de lady say, 'Tell Mrs. B. I very much obliged to her; and, (in a low and indifferent tone,) I thank you, Chloe, for bringing the parcel. So I lub my minister, and all Christian frien, dat try to do me good. I thank them: but I feel under very great obligation to God, who gib me de blessing, and make use ob his children to bring it to me."

Possessing a very humble opinion of herself, she compared her own mind, in distinction from others, to a very small vessel. Many, who were in the habit of meeting her in the little conference room, still remember with what animation she would break out, after having listened with delight to the conversation; and with hands uplifted, exclaim, --"O, my dear frien, I can wait no longer! My Gill Cup, (meaning that her capacity was so small it could contain but little, therefore, she must give vent to her feelings,) run ober, I mus speak few word." And from the fullness of her soul she would tell of the love of Jesus to poor sinners; expressing a deep sense of her unworthiness to make mention of his name, but saying that if she should hold her peace, the stones would cry out.

Conscious of her own weakness, with much feeling and simplicity, she would often advert to the exercises of the Psalmist, as those she wished to cultivate in her own bosom. 'Lord, my heart is not haughty, nor mine eyes lofty: neither do I exercise myself in great matters, or in things too high for me,' &c. "Yet I mus speak for my dear Saviour. De dead, praise not de Lord, but while Chloe lib, she mus praise him. She mus speak ob de glorious majesty ob his kingdom, and talk ob his power. All his works praise him, and his saints bless him. Chloe mus bless him too; my dear frien mus bear wid me if I speak too much."

In view of the mysteries and mercies of Providence towards her, she would exclaim, "I may say wid de Psalmist, 'I am a wonder to many.' Think what God done for poor me! So vile, so sinful, yet Jesus stoop so low, pick me up! Though I poor stranger, he pity me."

The first eight verses of the 56th chapter of Isaiah, were very precious to her; particularly from the 3rd to the 7th verse. "Neither let the son of the stranger, that hath joined himself to the Lord, speak, saying, The Lord hath utterly separated me from his people, &c. For, even unto them will I give in mine house and within my walls, a place and a name better than of sons and of daughters. Even them will I bring to my holy mountain, and make them joyful in my house of prayer." On these words she would expatiate with evident motions of heart-felt gratitude. And this was done with so much unaffected sincerity, that tears have often flown from the eyes of those who heard her. Indeed, the heart must have been hard, that did not swell with admiring and devout acknowledgment of the power and efficacy of divine grace, so clearly demonstrated before them. Said a Christian visiter, after hearing her remarks for the first time, "She is black, but comely."

It was with reluctance that she left the place of social worship, and the company of Christians. When the usual hour for closing a meeting arrived, she would console herself and others with the thought, that "in heaven, no nine-o'clock bell would hurry them home. No nine o'clock dare. Dat congregation neber break up."

She manifested much gratitude to God for the blessings of a quiet home, where she could, on her return from public worship, sit down alone, and meditate on the holy Scriptures; spread out her wants before God, and plead for fresh and more enlarged discoveries of his love to her soul.

With all her efforts, she was never able to read very correctly, though she made out to read the Bible, and some other good books, with such accuracy as to derive from them much satisfaction and spiritual improvement. And by close and constant attention, her mind was richly stored with Scripture knowledge. She retained a very grateful remembrance of those friends who instructed her, particularly Mr A. who also retained a Christian friendship for her, while she lived.

For a number of years she suffered exceedingly from rheumatic affections, which usually attacked her in the winter, and confined her for weeks, and sometimes months. Some of her fingers were drawn double with the violence of the disorder. Under those trials, she was patient, and submissive to the will of her heavenly Father; always justifying his dealings with her, and rejoicing that she was under his government. On recovering so as to be able to participate again in the public worship and ordinances of God's house, she seemed filled with gratitude and holy joy; and increasingly desirous of improving those dispensations in a suitable manner.

In the autumn of the year 1814, as was said of the patriarch, the time drew near that she must die; and having seasonably adjusted all her temporal affairs, her only concern was to be enabled to glorify God in her last sickness and death. This desire was happily fulfilled.

The following is extracted from a short memoir of her, which was published in the Massachusetts Baptist Missionary Magazine, a few weeks after her decease. It was written by Dr. Baldwin, who was then the editor of that work.

"Several of the last years of her life, her mind appeared uncommonly spiritual. As she advanced in life, she seemed to ripen for glory. Few Christians with whom we have been acquainted, have appeared to maintain so near a walk with God, or to enjoy so much of heaven.

"During her last sickness, which was of several months continuance, she was favoured with an almost uninterrupted peace of Mind. When exceeding low, she would frequently, while bolstered up in her bed, converse for hours with her friends who surrounded her, until her strength was quite exhausted. She improved every opportunity to exhort her Christian friends to walk worthy of the Lord, and to live in love and peace with each other. Such as she had reason to believe were in a state of unbelief, she most faithfully and solemnly warned to flee from the wrath to come. Many could not refrain from tears, while listening to her broken, but pious and moving exhortations. In one of the last visits made her by her Pastor only a day or two before her death, she observed to him, she had several times thought herself going to her blessed Saviour: but added, she was willing to stay or go, just as her heavenly Father should see fit to order. After a number of very touching observations, she said, "O, sir, I have been thinking of that blessed passage of Scripture, where it is said, 'They that be planted in the house of the Lord, shall flourish in the courts of our God. They shall bring forth fruit in old age. They shall be fat and flourishing; to show that the Lord is upright.'[*]

* "A funeral discourse was delivered from this passage by the Pastor of the church, the Lord's day following her interment."

This, sir, seems to be my experience. O, the Lord is good to me, poor unworthy creature." Death had no terrors for her. She seemed wholly resigned to the will of God, and, like good old Simeon, ready to depart in peace.

"On the 3rd of January, 1815, she gently fell asleep in Jesus, aged, as was supposed, about 65: and on the 7th, her remains were committed to the family vault of her former master, which was kindly offered by the heirs.

"She left by will to her grandson, $500. To five persons of colour, all members of the same church, $50 each; and to three of them, all her wearing apparel, beds, bed and table linen, and several smaller legacies to others. To the church, she gave $333,33 cents, the interest to be applied to the relief of the sick and poor, particularly to the members of colour. The remainder she left to the Baptist Missionary Society. She had previously made a present to her Pastor of $100."

Her funeral was attended by many of the members of the church; several of the family of Mr B. (who appeared to esteem it a privilege to have her bones deposited in the same tomb in which rested those of their fathers, and in which they anticipated laying their own,) besides various other persons, among whom, was the late Rev. Thomas Paul, whom she was much in the habit of calling her son.

Thus repose the ashes of CHLOE SPEAR, in the Granary Burial-Place, which borders on the Park Street meeting-house, in Boston.

And, when the trump of the arch-angel, shall issue its tremendous sound, ARISE, YE DEAD, AND COME TO JUDGMENT, who will be unwilling to appear in company with this lowly saint?

If it will be important at that solemn period to be found among those who have "washed their robes and made them white in the blood of the Lamb," let us "now, in the accepted time, and day of salvation," seek an interest in Him who is "the Resurrection and the Life;" for on such alone, "the second Death shall have no power." Such only will be "CHRIST's at his coming."

PRUDENCE, is a distinctive mark of a consistent Christian. For a woman professing godliness, to attempt, frequently, to have religious meetings conducted at her house, while her husband is pursuing a course that must interrupt their solemnity and order, would be no proof of sincere and humble engagedness in the cause. We therefore cannot avoid the conviction, that however gratifying it might have been in some respects, it was a dictate of wisdom to submit to the deprivation, in preference to subjecting the cause of religion to unfriendly observation. But now, finding herself alone, in the hope that her own growth in grace might be promoted, and that her neighbours and

others might be benefited; to see her throwing open
the doors of her dwelling, and inviting the friends of
the Redeemer to unite with her in acts of devotion
and praise, affords additional evidence, of her
Christian fidelity, and a love for souls. The
unassuming manner in which she received and
entertained those who honoured her, and gratified
themselves with a friendly interview, shows that
religion had a practical influence on her spirit and
conduct. What a happy world would this be, were
all its inhabitants actuated by the same principles
which governed this humble follower of her
Saviour!

The ingenuousness and pleasantry apparent in
the habit alluded to, of indulging her friends in a
little amusement when she uttered herself in her
broken style, differed widely from the irritability of
some persons, who injure the feelings of their
friends by resenting some trifling observation,
dropped without the least intention of wounding the
individual who has thus committed a little mistake,
and which, if turned off with an easy good-natured
smile, would at once discover an amiable
disposition, and save many painful sensations to the
parties concerned.

In the character before us, we see too, that the
religion of Jesus Christ expands the heart. It was
love for perishing souls, that brought him from
heaven to earth, to die for their redemption. And the
same love shed abroad in the hearts of his people
disposes them to acts of benevolence, and makes

them anxious for the salvation of their fellow-sinners. Having themselves tasted that the Lord is gracious, they desire that others should participate in the same blessing. It was this spirit that caused Chloe to sympathize with the afflicted, and to distribute her charities among the poor, and those who did not enjoy the privileges of the gospel; deducting from her own comforts, for the sake of theirs.

It was perfectly right and proper that she should cherish a grateful sense of the kindnesses rendered her by her valued benefactor, Mr Adams, and others of her friends, who had assisted her in the acquisition of useful and religious knowledge. It is not, however, always the case that persons do this. "The chief butler," we are told, (Genesis 40th) "did not remember Joseph, but forgot him," notwithstanding he was deeply indebted to him for services performed while under peculiarly trying circumstances, which to a grateful heart, renders a favour doubly valuable. And notwithstanding, the moving entreaties of Joseph, that he would remember him, when, as he assured him, he would be reinstated in a prosperous and desirable situation. But Chloe, it appears, enhanced the worth of favours shown her, by returns of gratitude, And by thus doing, she had a two-fold enjoyment.

And, how superlatively delightful must it have been to her, after arriving at her heavenly home, to welcome thither her esteemed friend, who had pointed her to the Lamb of God, under his earthly roof! And no less so, surely, to him, to find her safe within the walls of the New-Jerusalem, clothed in the "long white robe of the Redeemer's righteousness!"

"Blessed are the peace-makers," said our divine Lord. Happy, then, will it be for all those who possess and cultivate this amiable characteristic. And if, with all the disadvantages under which this poor African laboured, she acquired it, who need despair of inheriting those blessings, if sincerely disposed to promote harmony and good feeling among their fellow-beings?

Her usefulness in seasons of religious revival, is a subject of admiration, and should call forth our thankfulness to Him, who can even "take worms, to thresh mountains." The feeblest child of God may be useful at such times, if rightly influenced. But it must be confessed, that no common share of prudence is required in treating the case of an anxious sinner. It was not by pushing herself forward, and conversing, in a boisterous, dictatorial strain, as if she could tell a soul how to convert itself, that Chloe made herself useful. It was by gently administering the sincere milk of the word, in a kind, unassuming manner, as they were able to bear it, that she led along those who were inquiring after truth; and by tender and pathetic representations of the sufferings and compassion of the Saviour, that she won them over to a love of his character.

She was also a worthy example in having seasonably adjusted her temporal affairs! How many have neglected this important concern until they were so unwell as to be unable to attend to it, or perhaps until it was altogether too late. Consequently much trouble has ensued to survivors.

The sick bed,--the dying scene, --the triumphant departure--speak for themselves. And in view of them, how can any one refrain from saying, "Let me die the death of the righteous, and let my last end be like hers!"

It is sometimes objected to memoirs and narratives, that they present to view those parts of the character only, that were correct and praise-worthy; while they say nothing of its defects. In relation to this, we remark, that the preceding pages were not written with any idea of giving a perfect character. None such exists. The wise man asserts, that "there is not a just man upon earth, that lives and sins not." In common with all others, she was a depraved creature. None would be more ready to write TEKEL, (wanting,) against all their performances, than would have been our departed friend. Perhaps, however, as little could be brought forward, by any who knew her, that would go to sully a Christian profession, as in most cases that can be named. And while we fully agree with herself, that she was a "poor sinner," we feel the most undoubting assurance, that she was a sinner SAVED, by unmerited, distinguishing GRACE.

With the desire that "being dead, she may yet speak forth the praise of Him, who called her out of darkness into his marvellous light," this little monument has been erected.

The prayers of the reader are affectionately solicited, that the blessing of God, may cause it to be instrumental of good to many. And let all into whose hands it may come, be led by its perusal, to feel more tenderly for oppressed and benighted Africans; that so they may employ their influence and their property, in the advancement of all proper measures for their improvement. Then, millions of the sons and daughters of Africa, who are now as defenceless, and unenlightened, as Chloe once was, will be taught to read "the holy Scriptures, which are able to make them wise unto salvation."

> "Let every kindred, every tribe,
> On this terrestrial ball,
> To CHRIST all majesty ascribe,
> And crown Him, LORD of all."

CONCLUSION.

The subject of Slavery affords a melancholy evidence of the wickedness of man. It is probably true, that almost ever since this fallen world has been peopled, especially since the replenishing of the inhabitants of the earth after the general deluge some portions of our race have been held in bondage by others.

We are permitted, however, to rejoice in the power and grace of God, who, notwithstanding the depravity of human nature, has, in his infinite wisdom, so overruled and controlled events, as to make even slavery an indirect means of great good. Without any design on the part of those who have been engaged in the traffic, thousands, perhaps millions, have been brought under the sound of the gospel, and have repented, believed, and become the freeborn children of God. Multitudes of them, and among this happy number, our friend CHLOE, of whom we have just been reading, are at this moment, we trust, bowing with the holy company above, before the throne of the Eternal. Many more will yet be welcomed in that happy world, while some, perhaps many, of those who have been their oppressors on earth, will be forever shut out!

AFRICA, we believe, was born to be free. The time will come, when she will stand forward, an independent and enterprising nation; and will take an active and an honourable part, in advancing the interests and the increase of the Redeemer's kingdom. Notwithstanding the dullness and inaptitude of numbers of that people, which has led some persons to conclude that they could never be instructed to any considerable extent; there have, from time immemorial, appeared instances, which have afforded reason to determine, that there may be as great a capital of mind, in a given portion of that race of man, as in an equal number of other nations; and that under early and proper cultivation, detached, in the first place, from local disadvantages, and the contaminating influence of degrading society, would shine with equal lustre. Chloe was one instance. Early moral and physical culture, with kindly encouragement, and affectionate prompting, would probably have done wonders in her case; and so of thousands of others.

The efforts now making for the civilization of Africa, and for spreading the gospel in that populous country, inspire the confidence, that God is about to fulfil the gracious promise, so long since made to his saints;--"Ethiopia shall soon stretch out her hand unto God." In all succeeding ages, from that time to the present, his people have been praying for its accomplishment. And now, in his own set time, He, with whom "a thousand years is as one day," He, who "is wonderful in counsel and excellent in working," --is bringing about his own designs, and raising up instruments to effect his purposes; and happy are they who have a part assigned them in this work of benevolence.

Nor is it presumptuous to indulge the belief that the story of CHLOE'S conversion to God, her useful life, her peaceful death, may yet be used in the hand of the great Architect as a "pin" in supporting the fair fabric he is now constructing, to show forth the honour of his name! Her sainted spirit may, in the rolling ages of eternity, attune her immortal lyre, to anthems of praise unto Him, who not only has washed her from her sins in his own blood, but has rendered the knowledge of his abounding mercy towards her, instrumental of saving some precious souls, now perhaps, dwelling on the spot, where once stood the hut of her father! or on the woody beach, which echoed with her cries, when the hard-hearted man-stealer stifled her feeble voice with his handkerchief! Such, with the blessing of God, may be the happy results, when this little volume shall have been read in her native land.

Her feet being now planted on the shores of immortality, beyond the reach of oppressors, or the fear of invaders, she rejoices, triumphant through HIM, who hath made her more than a conqueror! There, at perfect liberty, and without interruption, she

> "Will range the blest fields,
>   on the banks of the river,
>   And sing HALLELUJAH,
> FOREVER AND EVER"

Printed in Great Britain
by Amazon